IGH SHERIFF O MERTHYR

Igh Sheriff o Merthyr

Mike Jenkins

First published in: 2023

ISBN: 978-1-84527-939-4

CYNGOR LLYFRAU CYMRU
BOOKS COUNCIL of WALES

Published with the financial support of the
Books Council of Wales

Cover design: Eleri Owen
Cover photo: Robert Haines

Published by Gwasg Carreg Gwalch,
12 Iard yr Orsaf, Llanrwst, Wales LL26 0EH
tel: 01492 642031
email: books@carreg-gwalch.cymru
website: www.carreg-gwalch.cymru

Dedicated to Al, Andrew & Jazz ...
friends through everything

ACKNOWLEDGMENTS – 'Pinch' journal (USA); 'Blue Oranges' anthology (Scotland); Culture Matters; 'Fish Rots From The Head' (e-book); 'Merthyr They Wrote'; 'Where we are now' website ed. Carol Ann Duffy; Red Poets.

Contents

BACK T NORMAL

My air's so long
I do look like an eavy metal band.
I carn walk proplee
coz of all-a letters
I ewsed t wipe my arse with.

I feel like I bin stranded
on some desert islan'
on'y without the sea
an them baboons
(some o the neighbours, mind ...).

Carn bleeve I aven murdered nobuddy,
not even the missis
oo made me wash my lips
b'fore kissin er goodnight.

Well, least we never goh it,
not like tha nurse up-a street
oo ad a bard dose
an nobuddy clapped f Boris,
not even them racists opposite.

Now things 're back t normal
I cun go back
t slaggin off the neighbours
an talkin about things tha matter
like the footie an lottery winners.

WE EWSED T GO

This is the way we ewsed t go
over t Swonzee Road,
on'y it's blocked by Trago.

Yew carn put no fence
t stop all them memrees,
like courtin on-a Sundiy –

we'd walk and-in-and
an lissen t the radio,
musta bin the top 20.

Aven bin yer frages
too scared I s'pose
since she passed away.

I wan'ed t find a path
not them metal spikes
an a notice 'bout securitee.

I'd feel er skin on mine –
now there's a warnin sign,
through-a gap tha toytown store.

We sung along t the Beatles,
Small Faces, Kinks an Stones –
er voice clear as birds in edgerows.

The roads 're all emtee
an shops full o fear –
wish I could walk er ome once more.

WE'RE FRONTLINE TOO

Goh gloves buh no mask.
It's right tha doctors 'n' nurses
get so much praise,
buh we're frontline too
standin at-a tills all day
f ardly no pay.

Mos customers 're okay,
buh some come an complain
yew aven goh this goh tha
an I carn do nothin
'cept nod an agree.

It don' elp t think
of all-a ways
the virus could pass on –
sometimes they're too close
an splutter an cough,
sometimes I wonder
ow many germs on cash.

Big shops like Deb'nams closin down
an I fear f'r-a fewture
in a town so pooer
an should my young daughter
plan t get outa yer.

A thanks an smile, larf an banter
keeps me goin f dayz arfta.

WHERE AVE ALL-A PIJINS GONE?

(**i.m. Wayne-O Pijin**)

Tha could easily be a song.
Carn say I miss em.
I wen down town t'day
jest t get some money
an never seen one!
Greggs is closed see
an ardly no chippies –
nobuddy spewin up weekends
s wha they goh t eat?
Ewjully I geh dive-bombed
jest walkin in-a bus station
an a presink's full of em
like gangs o mugger-birds.

They gone back t the woods?
Ave they yeard KFC's open
an 're pouncin on flung cartons?
They changed theyer diets
t eatin berries an leaves?

They'll be back, sure as rats,
sure as pasties. I never seen
no anorexic pijins yet.
All them spikes never stop em –
I reckon they're plannin
military manoeuvres f'r-a new bus station.

OWER VOICES

People slag off this town
say it int goh nothin,
jest fightin an drugs
an shops shut down.

Buh I know different see,
even though I wanna leave
t study, discover so much –
oo sayz I won' come back?

Me an my mukkas we tried
really ard at school
despite bein called 'swots',
didn wan' no dreary life.

All ad ower own dreams
some with art an mewsic
seen theirselves as Manics,
others like modern Trevithicks.

Teachers tol us we could do it,
made us bleeve in owerselves –
free meals an Council estates,
nothin could keep us down.

Now everythin as bin changed
by some blydi algorithm.
it's more like class war.
We're ripped up, flung on-a floor.

Buh we chanted down-a Bay
an them politicians give way –
provin the voices o the young
could be strong as any storm.

THIS IS MY OME

Ardly any like me up this valley,
buh even in Ponty there's a protest t'day.

I int one f politics mind,
all's I know is I carn get a job.

My girlfren's doin well in a shop,
lucky it's bin open this virus goin on.

Same day it's all kickin off,
statue pulled down an trouble in London –

I'm jest walkin down-a Igh Street
when these boyz I don' know shout out –

'Ey yew, geh back where yew come from!'
They wuz larfin an actin ard.

'I on'y live up-a road!' I replies,
they jest give me wanker signs.

Mos people yer are tidee, one ol marn
tol me about this Paul Robeson –

some black singer supported-a miners,
never learnt nothin 'bout im in school.

This is my ome, buh even b'fore lockdown
nothin wuz movin, nothin appnin.

MERTHYR MASS TESTIN

I ad a mask on
ee couldn yer me proplee –
'We goh mass testin in Merthyr see.'

'Wha?' ee wuz totelee gobsmacked,
'Where's tha? Wha's appnin?'
'Down Rhydycar, army's elpin.'

'Tha's totelee disgustin!' ee sayz
is eyes poppin out weird.
'In public, in front o ev'ryone?'

'Yeah, ev'rybody's doin it
speshly the older ones,
it'll be in an out quick.'

'Well I int, it's umiliatin mun!'
'Ow d'yew mean, yew cun find out.
They don' it up Liverpool.'

'Masturbatin? I've yeard it all.
Yew're avin me on!
Noh even in this town!'

WHILE THEY WOZ PARTYIN

While they woz drinkin wine in number 10 –
workin see, jest workin;

I woz sittin outside Dandelion Care Ome
wavin t my ol marn.

Ee couldn ardly see us
(fee knew oo we woz).

While they woz larfin an jokin,
my ol marn ad no companee.

We tried t mouth ellos,
didn know what t say.

Is eyes more distant ev'ry week,
tears as we touched-a window desperate.

While they woz takin-a piss,
p'lice outside doin nothin;

my ol marn died in is sleep
an on'y a few t bury im.

Ee worked f Oovers arf is life
till they closed it down.

Ol frens an work-mates lined-a streets
clappin as is earse wen' by.

In Downin Street theyer glasses raised.
Me an-a missis eld is wake in-a kitchen.

DON' KILL YEWER NAN

Don' kill yewer Nan this Chris'mas,
don' gob when yew talk to er,
meet up in-a ail, rain or snow
shout to er through-a window,
chuck er a spare drum-stick
out onta the pavement,
don' play Monopoly it'll cause
more arguments involvin spit,
make er sit in-a yard
pull a cracker with erself,
yew're doin er a favour
by totelee ignorin er.
Don' kill er with a cwtsh,
a peck's like an and grenade,
tell er yew'll see er proplee,
arfta the vaccine, later or soon ...
or jest teach er ow t ewse Zoom!

SMILO

Afto say I 'member im bes' pissed
off–of is ead at staff do's
eatin paper table cloths
or bombin-a Boss with bread rolls,
up on-a tables singin songs
till we goh banned from ev'ry pub.

Now ee've 'passed away'
(why don' they jest say 'dead' …
they scared or summin?) –
los track of im f yers,
ewsed t see im walkin is dog.

In-a compnee they called im 'Smilo'
coz ee wuz always grim (classic Merthyr),
when sober ee'd sit an say nothin.
At is weddin ee grinned with is bes marn,
looked awkward with is new missis.

Buh when ee'd ad a few
it woz like ee'd come out,
totelee different person,
never did get promotion –
guess the Boss wern impressed.

Big Catholic ee woz, Irish famlee
from Cork like the rest o them,
drawn by-a magnet o iron.
Musta bin bard, stopped goin t church –
priest come late coz o Covid.

OWER TORY CANDIDATE

'I'm votin Tory butt!
Seen er, standin f'r the 'ssembly?
She's a blydi eero
served in the army,
jest wha we need …
an they give us Brexit.

Don' care if she come from London,
lives in Gloucestershire
an ave never bin t Merthyr …
she've done trainin up-a Beacons.'

'So wha about Covid cock-ups,
factrees closin coz o Brexshit
all them blydi cuts
an corruption worthy o Trump …
anyway, it's the Senedd!'

'Don' matter, she've ad a life
not like them poncy pol'tishuns
down-a Bay, she'd give us
plenty o discipline an rools.'

'On'y the other day
yew wuz slaggin off Drakeford
coz yew couldn get down-a pub
an nobuddy could go t football.'

'Aye, but look at Thatcher,
she goh things done ...'

'Closed-a mines, give us-a poll tax,
sol off ev'ry industree on-a cheap,
couldn give a toss
'bout the likes o yew an me!'

'Know wha? Reckon yew're sexist!'

NOH OUTSIDE ENOUGH

(i Jamie Bevan)

Blydi ell, yew wouldn bleeve it!
Jest as we're comin outa lockdown,
ower Council closes this caffi down.

I ewsed t go there f breakfast,
I could try t practice the Welsh
I mos'ly forgot, t be onest.

My Nan woz totelee fluent,
buh all I remember are
'Cau dy deg!' an 'Nos da.'

Anyway, they goh an outside area
where I bin over las summer,
buh now it's noh outside enough.

It's cold when it's cold weather
an when the wind blows in,
buh apparently we need t be soppin.

We need ail on ower pice ar y maen
(learnt tha from Jamie oo runs it),
rain on coffee, snow on fried eggs.

Blydi ell, yew wouldn bleeve it!
While Spoons take over Penderyn Square,
theyer rools 're throttlin wha's yer.

OL PHIL REMEMBERED

It's sad when anyone dies,
apart from my ol marn
oo wuz a right bastard
piss-artist wife-batterer
Gran' Slam celebrator.

Ol Phil wuz quite a character,
ewsed t be in-a Navy
an ee'd go up-a reservoir
with all is medals on
t salute the yachts passin.

Ee loved the countryside
an-a 'Merthyr' ad two whool pages
praisin im (mind, I seen im
shootin birds an untin foxes
jest outside-a village loadsa times).

Ee once tol this young female solicitor
down-a Courts she oughta
'Stop soliciting here
and go down Burton's Corner!'
No ewse er complainin.

It's sad when anyone dies,
mind all them people ee sent down
f doin all them things
ee got away with no problem
wern exactly in mournin.

CHARLIE BOI

Charlie Boi lives up Cefn
ewge ouse like a manshun,
local celebritee always on-a telly
bangin on 'bout is lovely trees
an ow ee cares f'r animals.

Some locals treat im like royalty
coz of is MBE an ee gives em
Chris'mas dinner ev'ry year free
in-a village all. "Ooo tha Charlie,"
they d' say, "ee's soooo kind!"

Int so generous to is staff mind,
on pittance pay, though there's one guy
local writer name o Gray
follows im round like a corgi,
even speaks Welsh ... ee's on a lead.

President of a wildlife charitee
buh ewsed t be fox-untin on is land
an yew're noh tellin me
is cows an lambs don' end up
as Sundiy roasts with gravy.

Knew this bloke arrested f fishin
up Charlie's estate, gotta big fine.
Even goh is own eraldree
with an oak an a deer –
fee seen one, ee'd reach f is gun!

IGH SHERIFF O MERTHYR

Ee wuz off of is trolley,
shoutin in-a middle o Penderyn Square
like ee woz a Town Crier.

Ee ad all the regalia –
chains, fancy at, medals galore,
buh ardly spoke posher.

"Yer ye, yer ye! Good folk o Merthyr!
I'm yewer bran'new Igh Sheriff
appointed arfta givin bagsomoney.

Ower good Queen 've sadly
passed away, wavin from-a sky
on a separate cloud to er ubby.

She ave served us mos graciously,
same time lookin arfta er famlee
(speshly er darlin son Andy).

Now we welcome King Charlie III
oo once spoke sev'ral words o Welsh
an loves talkin t trees.

We say 'Croeso!' t Wills ower prince
an look forward t showin im round
b'fore ev'ry business shuts down town.

As Igh Sheriff I yerby decree
Prince Charles becomes King Charles ospital
an Keir Ardie Ealth Centre's named arfta Camilla.

As Igh Sheriff I yerby declare
this square will enceforth be named arfta me –
Josiah John Bacon Homfray Crawshay."

JWBILI STREET PARTY

Wen' t this street party
up the end o Shirley
(my ol butty sayz
'Ow come they name a street
in this once iron-town
arfta some ancient film star?').

It wuz all done up fancy –
buntin galore an Ewnion Jacks,
loadsa pictures o Lizzy
an even 'Republicans are welcome'
on a small sign out the way.

There woz Victoria sponge
an Coronation Chicken sandwiches
buh no sign o Jwbili Puddin,
though there woz a custard dish
the colour o Boris's air.

It woz mos'ly drinkin an eatin
an an attempt at 'God Save the Queen'
which set off the local dogs
owlin like blydi banshees.
Coupla ol Vets wearin medals.

Till this bloke come along –
sayz ee carn geh out of is ome,
sayz ee put in an objection,
sayz the Council ignored im,
moanin 'bout is freedom.

Wha's ee on about, eh?
Tomorrow we'll geh back
t payin all ower blydi bills
an queuin t see the doctor.
'Ave a drink mun, sit down!'

Buh all ee done wuz go on
'bout oo killed Diana, Andrew's crimes,
all this stuff about Onours.
Steve, oo's a bouncer, soon sorted im.
Wern even from round by yer.

CELEBRATIN SHAKEY

Ave yew yeard,
on World Book Day
we goh an Ol Shakey Festival
appnin in Merthyr?

Celebratin tha great writer
(no, noh Shakin Stevens)
buh the marn oo give us
Fluellen an Glendower.

The bes thing tha's goin on
ull be in Penderyn Square,
where loadsa school kids
will stage an ewge battle
jest like-a Capulets an Montagues.

On'y this time it'll be
the Ouse o Ewitt v. Ouse o Windsor
led by Arry an William lookalikes,
two gangs beatin-a shit
outa each other,
jest like a Saturdiy night.

There'll be no Romeo from-a Gurnos
meetin Juliet from Lakeside Gardens –
an ol-fashioned punch-up
till 'mergency services break it up
an standin in-a may'em
Chief Inspector Escalus sayz –
"A plague on both yewer Ouses!"

THE KING IN OWER TOWN

Ee spoke t me
like ee wuz ordinree,
ee ... me? ...
spoke ... I couldn bleeve,
im ... King Charles Three
sayz "Hello!"
like I woz somebuddy
an I'm on'y ...
an ee's so ...
I wuz totelee gobsmacked
I wuz jest wavin
my little Ewnion Jack
an one of an undred
"You don't need to bow!"
"Your Maj ..." ee moved away,
in ower small town
im ... yer ... in-a presink
walkin by-a charitee shops
up t the Red'ouse,
now I feel really important
well, for a moment –
I adto go back
t my blydi freezin flat
with fuckall t eat –
buh f a few seconds
felt like a celebritee,
me ... im ... royalty –
such a proper gent.

WHARRA BOI!

Wharra boi tha Arry, eh?
left is famlee's big ouse up Cefn,
buggered off t the States
with a woman o colour.

On'y wrote a book, dinee?
Slaggin off is brother
an is ol marn Charlie
oo's runnin-a famlee compnee.

Some sayd ee wuz on'y
tryin t make a fortewn
talkin on-a radio an telly
ow is brother panned im out.

Bes bit woz ow ee lost is virginity
in-a field near the Abersarn Inn
t this older woman
(ev'ryone knows er round town).

Wharra boi, eh?
Fought in Afghanistan
an killed loadsa them rag-eads
(tha's wha ee called em).

Ewsed t go untin up Ponstic
when ee woz young.
Pretty soon they're makin Charlie
a Free Marn o the Town.

I don' reckon Arry'll be yer
t celebrate. I reckon
ee might ave an accident ...
jest like is mam done.

THA OL DEPUTEE

First time frages I seen im
tha ol Deputee
walkin down-a Igh Street
strugglin with a walkin-stick.

This bloke shouts out to im –
'Ey Loopy! Loopy-O!'
Ewsin tha familiar nickname
ev'ryone done at school.

The Deputee Geoff squints
across at the marn,
tryin t move on quickly,
buh ee wern avin it.

''member me? Darren?
Yew didn arf gimme one
straight in-a chops
an I wern doin nothin.'

'I'm sorry, I don' seem ...'
'Yeah, yew woz a right twat 'en!'
Darren seen is butty, moved on –
'Whapnin Goj? Pint 'en?'

The Deputee Geoff excaped.
I 'member blood an screamin
parents up-a school tampin,
ow nothin come of it.

I SEEN IM

Im! Seen im up Cyfarthfa Park,
yew know tha specky twat
of a politishun, woz ee arfta
some Charlie or wha?
Maybe ee'd yeard this is
the bes time f ower magie crop.

Some woman presents im
with lovely Merthyr oney,
fee wuz closer I'd-a give im
the ol Swonzee Road kiss,
as it woz all I could manage
wuz a swift V-sign.

Fuckin Tories eh, wha they doin
in a town like this?
Coal an iron gone, noh much else,
people treated like piss –
bin forgotten too long.

We don' need no Crawshay,
blydi Guest or Bacon sorts –
jest a chance t show
wha we cun achieve.
Ee leaves, talkin 'bout is beautiful Ewnion,
which is broken, f'ever broken.

GOIN F GOLD

'Shoplifters on the way!'
The walkie-talkie tells me
on the tills at H 'n' B,
there's a run on turmeric –
why carn they jest
eat more blydi curry?

'One's got grey track-suit bottoms,
the other a black oodie.'
tha could be anybuddy
in this town. They're arfta oney,
top class stwff, Manuka.

Arfta raidin Icelan' f meat
they d' come yer. Fair play
they d' go f gold.
I see em, don' phone-a p'lice
'less they get stroppy.

It's ard even if yew're workin,
two kids an I'm a single mam.
Arf o them 're feedin abits
an I'm not talkin sugar addiction!

Bloke come in, grey trackies an oodie –
'Can I elp yew sir?'
'Yeah ... lookin f turmeric tabs, goh any?'

TOTELEE BEYOND

So I go down town shoppin
coz my gran'son's Under 7 game
as bin cancelled outa respect.

Loadsa people chattin an larfin
an mos o them noh wearin black –
felt like sayin – 'Ow cun yew smile?'

Met this fella I ewsed t work with,
thought ee wuz tidee
till ee started givin off –

'Wha's there t blydi respect butt?
She woz rich buh done nothin ...
jest appened t be born inta tha.

Ow many ol people ull die
this winter, freezin t death
or starvin or stuck on ospital trolleys?

Ow many will be given DNRs
jest coz they're over 70
an nobuddy gives a shit?

It's us an them mun –
the pooer an the rich, yew think
they care 'bout anythin cept wealth?

'Yew're totelee beyond!' I sayz
an eaded to-a pawnbroker
t cash my weddin ring.

MERTHYR IS SHUT

I wuz gunna cross-a walkway
over inta town, buh it's shut.

My kids love tha Splash Park
over Cyfarthfa, buh it's bin closed frages.

We ewsed t go swimmin down Rhydycar
buh the pool's still out of action.

Don' bother with-a libree no more
coz yew gotta book t get in.

When I found-a bran'new bus station
arf the services woz cancelled.

Red'ouse caff ewsed t be tidee,
buh there's bars 'cross the entrance.

I wen' t the Civic Centre t complain
buh it's noh open t the public.

So I wen' up our Member's office tampin
an this bloke at-a desk sayz – 'Shut it!'

TOO ARD T LEARN

See, Welsh is too ard t learn.
I wuz put off at school ...
all them mutants mun.
Carn speak a word!

                        Where to yew from?

Merthyr Tydfil, why yew askin?

                        Yew jest spoke it 'en.

Ow d'yew mean?

                        Wha's Merthyr mean?

Well, martyr, like-a team.

                        See! Where yew from in town?

Heolgerrig, up the ill.

                        Which means?

Rocky road, o course,
jest like them cakes.

                        There, yew don' it agen.

Don' wha mun?

                        Spoke it! Heolgerrig!
                        Ow 'bout yewer street name?

It's Durham Close.

                    Well, there's limits I s'pose.
                    Know any Welsh songs?

Aye, Sospan Fach an Calon Lan.

                    Yew don' need much
                    t carry on.

Pint o beer?

                    Peint o gwrw.

Sausage 'n' chips?

                    Selsig a sglodion.

Fuckin Tory scumbags?

                    Some things are best
                    left as they come.

IN-A WAITIN ROOM

In-a waitin room f A an E
ev'ryone sittin quiet
till this little girl starts singin
'Sospan Fach' an we open up.

In-a corner, a set o screens
with towel an blanket draped over,
as we wuz talkin ages, the girl 7
an others 70, suddenly
this ead pops up –
this bloke on a drip
declares – 'I'm 92!'
(ee wuz 'bout 40,
buh on summin!).

'Bin yer since Thursday!'
Is drip woz runnin out,
'No blydi beds see!'
Ee ad is own den.

Offered the girl a chocolate yoghurt
an er mam sayz she orready
wuz hyper on Coca Cola.

The screen-marn comes out,
tells ev'ryone ee's off f'r a fag,
walks pas'-a trolleys in-a corridor
each with a patient (now I know
why they d call us tha).

The little girl imitates puppies an dolphins
an we all larf an chat,
apart from-a woman in-a wheelchair
oo's white as bone, still as a memorial.

GIMME A BRAIN

I bin yer all night long
waitin is a skill see
don' ave no mobile phone

my daughter stayed with me
buh now she've gone –
she'll be back when a bed come

ewsed t work down-a Maerdy
things woz different then –
little ospital, steppin stone

ol people speshully ... then I forget
tha this is me an Ray ave passed away
few years ago, eart attack see

all of-a staff bin great,
tea an blood pressure endlessly –
I ardly slept a wink

lights on an the lady on a trolley
with er bag full o ev'rythin –
nurse oo give me a blanket

now I'm in a wheelchair ready
it's like a race is beginnin –
"Yew goh promotion!" Ray ud say

two new knees, ip nex opefully –
wonder if they'll gimme a brain,
so's I don' afto worry?

A 'N' E AGEN

I'm back in A & E agen,
done my arm in on-a scaffoldin,
carn afford t go on sick
buh it's too much pain –
surjree might as well be planets away.

Machines o crisps, coke 'n' chocolate
keep us goin.
This one fella moanin
'bout is swollen balls at Reception.
Woman nex to me
on the edge o summin –
"Yew don' give a fuck 'bout me!"
she tells er mam an dad concerned.

This other woman carn stop coughin –
nobuddy wears masks no more,
slike the whool thing
wuz jest a bard dream.

When they finlee call my name
"Joseph Mahoney" I ardly reco'nize
it's me, so long Joey.
Ope it int broken –
too much seems shattered nowadays –
ower town, my famlee.

I'M A MACHO MARN

Though my legs 're white as lambs
I ewsed t play in-a scrum –
wha'ever the weather
my airs 're showin –
see my boney knees
even when-a skin
goes blue as anti-freeze –
in-a snow, frost or storm
see my naked pins –
no jeans nor trousers f me
I'm ard as they come.
This bloke comes up t me
"Wha yew wear in summer butt,
a blydi furry at?"
Then ee starts singin
"I'm a lumberjack and I'm okay" –
like I woz wearin a dress or summin.

Don' ee know I'm the Bear Grylls
o the presink, explorin
Iceland (tha's the shop!).

BECOMIN A WOMAN

See, I wen f'r an interview
an they arst me
'Were you born a woman?'
I mean ... ow blydi crazee!
Tol em I woz born a donkey!

Tha's wha they do nowadays.
I know this fella
ee become a woman,
full op ee ad.
Lovely marn, s'licitor an all,
never slept with a woman.
Ee goh transferred totelee.
Mind, some with kids
end up doin–a same.

Buh wha would appen
if I fancy im ... er I mean.

Well, she've goh all equipment
down b'low, proplee fitted.

It's loop-the-loop,
sooner marry a donkey.

Yewer abits, I reckon
tha's far more likely.

TWO CONES

They ditched theyer ewsual ats
an dressed as traffic cones –
Mark 'n' Sharon, eeroes o town.

It woz theyer statement of-a times
where Cefn's become Cone City
an Eads of-a Valleys the same.

DE / TOUR it read on-a two of em
givin us a larf down-a presink,
sparkin ower drab dayz.

Bright orange, faces protrudin –
we need more like em,
ev'ryday crazee so speshul.

Wha'ever they become tomorrow –
cranes, cack or pesky pijins,
we'll welcome them.

LOST IN CEFN

Ne'mind 'Lost in France' or 'Lost in Translation',
ee wuz 'Lost in Cefn'.

First time at night
on-a Eads o the Valleys

or, as we now call it
Cone City Central.

Suddenly, ee takes a wrong turn
straight inta a nightmare.

Down an ill on a pot-oled track
ee knew summin woz up

when ee braked by a crane –
there woz arf a bridge above

an bright lights like warnins.
Fella in an ard at come up t im –

'Wha yew doin yer butt?'
'Sori ... I'm lookin f Merthyr!'

'Yew need t geh back on-a road ...
yew shouldn be yer.'

'Wish I wozn ... SATNAV's no elp!'
So ee turned an wen back,

soon found the main road, ee eaded
the same way ee'd bin comin!

AVENUE DE CLICHÉ

We're all sat yer waitin
f'r-a elp to arrive from up there,
summin like Oovers –

a bran'new factree become
loadsa o emptee buildins
perfect f demolishun.

Buh even if it come tomorrow
we'd all be too pissed or stoned
t do summin positive.

We all vote Labour o course,
even though mos of us
really couldn give a toss.

Drive round on mobility scooters
or wheelin shoppin bags,
as boy-racers fly past.

Forgettin ower ramblers,
runners, dog-walkers, cyclists
down-a Taff Trail an beyond.

We're all sufferin from too much istree –
slike dust in-a air ... mind, with opencast
I reckon it's still blydi there.

ARF-MARTIAN STAR TURN

We need t sign im up quickly
ee's arf Martian:
Dad's from Abercynon,
Mam the red planet.
ee's gonna become
the nex big thing,
I don' care if ee carn sing.

Tha one antenna'll do it
plus the revolvin ead,
the way ee changes inta dust
at the end o ev'ry song.
The crowds'll love it,
I cun see the album cover –
'The Valleys Own Rocket'!

Oo needs ewmans any more
with theyer many colours
an strange sexual abits?
Ee cun reproduce solo.
there is life on Mars
an ee as proved it
third eye a telescope.

We need t sign im up
with is Valleys-bleepin accent,
even though nobody'll understand
a single word of it!

EXECUTIN DISSIDENTS

They're shootin-a dissidents on the illside
Bang! Bang! Bang!
all blydi mornin
up the ol farm,
it's really disturbin
when yew're tryin t watch Andrew Marr
an arf-a Cabinet self-isolatin.

Gunfire on the Sabbath
they jes don' care,
carried 'cross-a Waun
like some militree manoeuvre
up Epynt Mountain.
I carn take no more.

I don' go t chapel
buh call myself a Christian
an they goh no respect.
They wanna execute them
on a workin day
when I'm noh in.

"It's clay pijins!" my missis insists,
buh I bin bingein on-a Andmaid's Tale
an I know wha's appnin.

NO ORDINREE EAT

I come back from workin on-a site
sweatin like a marathon runner at-a finishin line,
ave a cold shower, suck an ice-pop in one,
take a flannel out the freezer
t wrap around my goolies
an sit in front of a fan.

This int no ordinree eat.
If I woz in Costa Wha'ever
I wouldn mind under an umbrella
an knockin back-a lager,
buh this is Merthyr f fuck's sake.
I los three pounds up on-a roof.

Then my daughter breezes in
from er job in a phone shop
(all totelee air-conditioned),
takes one look at my beetroot face
sippin er ice coffee from Costa
an sayz – 'Dad, I'm totelee knackered!'

THE MARN AT STAN' 13

On-a ground
the former carpet fitter
sits at Stan' 13
avin a picnic
on-a 'Daily Mirror' –
is teeth ave disappeared
like mos of the buses,
ee gums a pastie
slurps some Coca Cola,
ewsed t own a shop
up Pontmorlais,
could cut a measure
like no other –
now is back's playin up
umbrella is is stick –
ee've laid-a floors
of all-a women
on-a bus up the ill –
don' need no dentures
t chops away.
News is the playground
is bein demolished f ousin
an ee's gobsmacked –
wife left im years back,
they still meet up
t go t chapel.

Nose thin as a Stanley knife,
skinny as skirtin boards.
Even-a grumpy drive
sayz is 'Goodbye!'
as ee struggles t gerroff –
pain like pummelin nails
the pavement's ard surface
shows no print or yield.

COZ I WOZ STARVIN

On'y stole coz I woz starvin
noh bin done f nickin b'fore

on'y stole one sandwich,
think it woz chicken

I int goh nothin –
cut my benefits, carn afford nothin

no jobs goin,
ones tha are int worth avin

Securitee ad me,
grabbed an pinned me

knee in-a back,
arm yanked up an killin

like I'd murdered somebuddy,
a psycho gone loopy

face t the ground
an a boot in the ead

in a nick I'll eat better,
an ave a tidee bed.

EEROES

See em down town more 'n' more
young people they're busy
trainin f the nex war.

They goh smart sweat shirts
an casual ewniforms, look ready
f'r a game or run.

Oo knows when it's gunna come –
will it be Russia, China,
or the riotin pooer?

All's I know is, it gives em
a sense o purpose an belongin,
one day learnin t kill f'r a livin.

They need youngsters like them
from famlees oo're always strugglin –
a tidee job with guarantees.

The same oo wen t Bloody Sundiy,
Basra an Baghdad, oo fought
in the name o the Queen, now King.

The same oo shot down innocent people
looked like frens. Call em Eeroes –
give em medals f'r all tha murd'rin.

MY EATIN POLICY

Is stoppin in bed all day long –
I aven done tha
since my oneymoon.
Buh now the missis ave gone
my on'y compnee
is the television.

Down town apparently
they goh summin called
an Eatin Bank,
it's where Wilko ewsed t be,
some fancy name like Talkin Shop.

Made my will the other day –
my ouse'll go t pay
f me in an Ome.
Sometimes it feels
like this bed's a comfy coffin
when all my joints pain an stiffen.

My kids goh me a mobile –
fair play they do ring
t check if I'm still livin –
"I've moved t Bedford"
I tell em an they larf
with "See yew soon!"

EY MISTER LAN'LOR'

Tell me, Mister Lan'lor'
wha yew doin t me?
Jest me an my kid
tryin t make ends meet.

I work like a dog
a collie chasin sheep,
I'm on yewer leash.
Carn afford no car,
train fares always goin up,
food prices beyond
'lectric's the same –
yew wan' us t end
up on-a street?

Ey Mister Lan'lor'
I know yew gotta make money,
buh yew goh more ouses
than I goh GCSEs
an I done tidee
even though I work up Trago.

Yew ever gone without?
Gone to a foodbank?
Secon' thoughts I'm more like a sheep,
with yew snappin us inta pens.
Wha's-a fewture, eh?
Some ewman blydi abbatoir?

WORK T BE DONE

Yew're blowin up-a mountain
creatin all tha dust –
yewer famlee breathin it in

buh oo cares mun?
there's money in jobs t be done

yew're slaughterin-a pigs an sheep
lettin em slowly bleed
f pies yew don' even eat

yew're stackin-a shelves
of a mock blydi castle
outside o town

buh there's money t earn
an jobs t be done

yew're makin them weapons,
yew don' know where they're goin –
the Saudis or Ukraine

buh it's on'y a job
an oo's askin questions?

yew're ammerin all-a doors
collectin debts from famlees
strugglin like yewer own

buh, f now, yew int bothered,
coz there's work t be done.

FLEEIN A MONSTER

She come on-a bus,
blood streamin down er face
from a gash on er fore'ead,
one black eye looked bard.

Somebuddy sayz – "Tha's the bes
Alloween make-up I seen yet!"
Then she bursts out cryin,
this woman give er a cwtsh.

"Whassa matter 'en love?"
"Ee've kicked me out!
Goin up my mam's I am …
Witch ee sayz, geh on yewer broom!"

The blood run down er t-shirt,
somebuddy give er tissues.
No party f'r er tonight,
fleein a real monster.

This bloke gehs on at-a Club,
scars an stitches, all kindsa stuff.
Nobuddy sayz nothin, as-a girl
olds er ead an weeps.

GIRLZ CARN PLAY

Girlz?
They carn play football!
More bothered 'bout make-up
an jewelree comin off,
theyer air disturbed,
theyer fake tans
messed up by bruisin.

Girlz?
All blydi lesbos anyway,
on'y geh involved
f'r-a changin rooms
an oo they fancy,
all affairs an intrigues
like 'Eastenders' on fields.

Girlz?
Well, I aven actually seen
any of-a games on telly,
buh I cun imagine em
doin theyer nails arf time.
Blokes that watch em
mus' be dead pervie.

OO STOLE OWER TOWN?

Somebuddy stole ower town centre!
Some say it could be idden
up-a Retail, or stuck inside
them cardboard walls o Trago.
Others reckon it's bin taken
down t Cardiff, buh the buses
would never come t carry it.

Somebuddy stole ower town centre
coz the shops keep disappearin
an theyer emptee as Tory brains –
the piss-artists all bleeve
it's bin shifted underground
an fills the ol mines.

Somebuddy stole ower town centre
an now the Council's tryin t find
film companees with apocalyptic movies
oo're lookin f perfect settin's.
Oo nicked it ... woz it Westmonster?
We're searchin f someone t blame
buh even-a Portuguese an Poles 're leavin.

WATCHIN-A MOULD

I watch-a mould grow
spreadin like a disease
in my boy's lungs
X-ray an I carn do nothin.
Over arf my pay
goes on-a rent –
wouldn call it ome,
jest a place t go
instead of-a street.

I cwtsh my boy in bed
so close an ope
ee don' geh worser
as ee's coughin bard.
Invite ower frens f tea –
rats 're gettin bigger by the day!

If my mam didn look arfta Kyle
I'd be totelee lost,
workin all owers on-a tills.
Money flows away
like-a Taff down valley,
t Cardiff an beyond.

Kyle cries – 'Mam ... I'm sooooo cold!'
an even in is dreams
ee carn excape ... is nightmares
o water rushin in an drownin.

KINDA DIED

It woz Merthyr fine dinin –
pizzas on plates noh boxes,
pasta in big bowls an a tree
growin in-a middle of a restront
(though it woz a fake one).

'Wha'ever appened t Colin?'
arst my missis to a fren
she hadn seen frages
(even though ee wuz sittin opposite).

I did reconize im
despite is total change
from a plump salesman
with dark air an no sign
o strayin from-a norm.

Missis thought ee wuz somebuddy else.
This sculptor called Feng Shoo
ee called isself – white air,
pointy beard an a mobile
fulla pitchers of is metal creations.

So is wife woz stunned,
buh Colin stroked is beard sayin –
'I kinda died see,
an come back t life agen …
£4000 grand per sculpture … noh bard goin!'

OL BOILERS

"We're all gettin ol see,
Ower boilers 're breakin down.
With me, it woz a combi I ad
years ago now, buh soon as the cold
spell come really bard
it woz my condenser pipe.
It woz jest like I couldn piss,
all tha gunge collectin
ad t be flushed out
like I ad a blockage in my tewbs.

When it was cut
I ad so much relief,
the water pourin out clean,
till they operated
an put a new gadget in,
never seen one b'fore,
musta bin on 'Dragons' Den'!

The ol boiler's better f now.
Still makes funny noises in-a mornin,
I cun ardly afford t keep it goin."

"Oh aye ... did yew ewsed
t work in central eatin?"

SHUTTERDOM

Goh shutters on the Igh Street
so many different colours
yew'd ardly bleeve.

Red, green, orange, grey,
it's a rainbow o closed down
shops, caffs an companees.

Now I'm the Igh Sheriff
I reckon we cun make a few pounds
outa all this dereliction.

Think Tobermory an Aberaeron
with theyer multi-coloured ouses
an trusty town brands.

We'll rename Merthyr 'Shutterdom' –
come an see wha ewsed t be,
meet the spirits o Ghost Town.

As Igh Sheriff I yerby decree
we're no longer Tragoville or Charityton.
Do it f tourism … Get Them Shutters Down!

OW 'BOUT?

Food banks.
warm banks.
baby banks.
kidibanks.
'magine wha's comin nex!

Teen banks.
middleagedcrisisbanks.
pensioner banks.
travel banks –
jes sit down as 'ey show
films o destinations.
Work banks –
collectin stwff f other banks.
Trouble is, these int banks.

'few wen inta a bank
sayin – "Gis some money f free!"
Yew'd be tol
where t go rapidly.

Ow 'bout a society
with no need f any o these?
Ow 'bout tidee jobs
which pay enough money?

Trouble is, mos people
ud afto go on blydi strike.
Now there's a tidee idea.

PICNIC IN A CAR

It's winter,
theyer avin a picnic
in theyer car agen,
im an er
up Cyfarthfa Park
overlookin-a lake
shaped like a fish
(local knowledge tha).

Ev'ry day they're there
with sarnies an flask
watchin ducks, swans, geese –
mus geh dead borin.

Loadsa layers o clothin
an they on'y goh a small car –
a wonder they fit in!

They ewsed t walk
round 'n round the lake –
one day changed direction.

Save on eatin bills,
keep breathin,
doze in the afternoon.

Spottin-a dog-walkers,
famlees with children,
opeful tourists an istorians,
an them anglers sittin
with rods ready,
patient as them.

MIDNIGHT RAPPER

On-a las train ome arfta the game
(which, o course, woz a bus!).

It'll be orright when we're dead
an-a bran'new Metro's sorted.

City fans chantin the ewsual
'Jack bastards!' an 'CCFC'.

Gettin on-a bus at Ponty
ee looked like a down-n-out –

bedraggled, pulled outa the Taff
on-a floodin night.

All of a sudden from-a back
thought I yeard shoutin.

Buh it woz im rappin
to them foorball fans.

Givin em the ol ands,
swearin an angry, as they woz larfin.

Till they get drawn in
by is attitude, is rhythms.

An they clap im till Abercynon.
Ee gets off at Aberfan.

Scarf bound round is ead,
disappearin inta stormy night.

WERN MY FAULT

There wuz this fuckin ard gang
led by this bloke Vlad
(arfta some ol rooler).

Ee didn give a toss
'bout trainers on wires,
ee wan'ed more terrortree.

We wern gunna take no messin,
ee knew t keep out –
we'd flash ower weapons.

No way ee'd risk it,
noh even with is boyz
all tooled up an ready.

Fancied isself ee did,
ewsed t ride orses bare-back,
shirt off, flobby flab.

Till one night they invaded
ower Igh Street askin f trouble,
shoutin theyer gobs off.

Joey goh stabbed, I cut
one of em 'cross is face
t stop im attackin.

It wern my fault see,
I woz on'y defendin myself.
P'lice wouldn lissen.

STEALIN JESUS

Somebuddy stole-a baby Jesus
from-a manger outside St. David's –
problee some piss artist
or one o them druggies.

It wuz found in-a Taff
floating down past-a weir,
goh stuck in a shoppin trolley
lookin in a bard way.

Vicar never bothered –
it ud lost a leg
an woz really manky
covered in muck, bed o cans.

Loads o people gathered
on-a walkway f photos
o Christ in-a river –
like it woz a celebritee.

Then one day, the water surges
an carries im away
t Cardiff like ev'rythin else –
coal, people, money.

GOIN F VLAD

We're goin f Vlad
we're gonna geh im
over-a walls
an inta the gardens.
Wha's ee doin yer anyway,
streets ee don' b'long
doin all kindsa deals?

Im an is boyz struttin
in ower terrortree
like 'ey owned-a place.
Buh now we're tooled up,
now we goh protection
Vlad'll be shakin.

An when we find im
we'll kick the shit
outa im an is mates,
we'll ammer em t the ground
put the boot in.
Is face ull be swollen up
an bleedin, bruises
the on'y medals
ee'll be wearin.

When ee's lyin there
in-a gutter where ee b'longs
is jaw an teeth broken,
on'y then we'll arsk im –
Vlad son, tell us wha yew wan',
we're all lissnin!

EMPEROR O CHINA

Ee wen round all-a pubs
one arfta another –
Wyndham, Narrow Gauge, Anchor,
even-a so-called cocktail bars
on'y open weekends.

They called im 'Z' f short.
Short f wha I dunno.
'I'm jest collectin' ee sayd.
Buh ev'ryone knew
ee always wan'ed summin.

If it wern is dues
it woz essenshul information
ee'd pay good money for
an offer protection
(always an eavy by im).

We on'y found out later
when we seen-a eadlines –
this marn found dumped in-a reservoir,
some bloke from-a Midlands,
talk o 'county lines'.

Ee come buyin drinks week arfta
like celebratin the orses or poker,
actin all innocent buh winkin.
My clever mate sayz –
'Tha's im ... Emperor o China!'

Note – 'China' was the name of a notorious slum area in 19th century Merthyr and its hardest man called the 'Emperor'.

BUS CATCHIN BLOOZ

So I woz waitin f'r-a bus
in ower bran'new bus station
with bran'new caff an bogz
yew hadda pay for,
even though nobuddy goh cash no more.

It woz miles late,
this bloke with an App
kept tracin it somewhere up-a Beacons,
ev'rybuddy moanin bout politishuns.

When it come arfta ages
driver goh off leavin them passengers
from Brecon locked inside
like they woz fish in a tank.
They squeezed gainst-a glass, bewildered.

Someone pushed a button t let em out.
Another bus arrived, driver goh off.
we all piled on in ope,
till this official from a companee
sayz it's cancelled, drive's goh Covid!
Wen up-a train station in desperation
an caught-a replacement bus.

Goh t Cardiff jest in time
t catch-a las bus ome.

BATS DO ROOL!

Bats do rool Merthyr!
Yew won' see tha in-a paper.

Noh the blydi Council
nor them politishuns.

They're the ones roostin
jest angin about waitin

f'r the moment t stop
the Merthyr Risin festival,

or the ol Rugby Club
becomin a venue.

The leader of ower Bat Party
Dusk Pipistrelle owns it all –

won' take no batshit
or others wingin it.

Int no vampires like them royals
suckin the money off of ev'ryone.

Viva Batman, Batwoman, Batwha'ever!
People 're like insects t them.

SALAD DAYZ

It's gotta be Monday
in this tired ol town
an Jazzy G's busy dealin
in the shaded alleyways.

Ee'll geh yew wha yew wan,
the ard stuff like cukes
or even them ripe cherries.

Buh t'day Big Al from over Irwin
is arfta summin speshul –
"Goh any beefsteaks mun –
I wan the real eavies?"

Jazzy G goh all the contacts
fancy growers an polytunnels,
a direct line t Morocco.

"Don' sell me no shit now!"
sayz Big Al sniffin a sample, takin a bite.
"I'm plannin an ewge party see.
Salad dayz mun, salad dayz!"

NATIONAL ALERT

I woz up my ol marn's
when-a 'larm wen off.

Ee's wha I d' call
an SM dinosaur.

Nothin t do with whips,
ee ates compewters an-ah.

Ee calls em all
dot-dot machines.

So my phone goes crazee
at 3 on-a sofa.

'Fuckin ell, wha's tha?'
ee shouts gobsmacked.

'Dad, it int nothin,
it's jest a newclear attack,

it on'y means tha Pewtin
ave pressed-a red button

an we goh a coupla minutes
t find a bunker or panic!'

Ee grins, takes another swig
of is can o lager

an calmly announces –
'Tha's why I goh no mobile see.'

WASTED YEARS

We've spent too many wasted years
thinkin 'bout wha ower neighbours
're thinkin 'bout us.

Always feelin inferior
when they buy new things,
ave lots o posh visitors.
Delighted when they give us a wave
from theyer convertible Jag.

Now, at las, we don' give a toss!
We're ol enough t go ower own way,
make ower own rools,
stop lookin over t see
oo's spyin through-a blinds.

Even called ower ouse
by a name they ate – 'Golygfa'r Waun' …
'What does that mean?' they arst.

Too many wasted years listenin
t them boastin 'bout
olidays in-a sun, villas across the world.

We look out on ower small garden
an see wha's growin.